How Can I Remember All That?

of related interest

Can I tell you about ADHD?
A guide for friends, family and professionals
Susan Yarney
Illustrated by Chris Martin
ISBN 978 1 84905 359 4
eISBN 978 0 85700 708 7

Can I tell you about Dyslexia?
A guide for friends, family and professionals
Alan M. Hultquist
Illustrated by Bill Tulp
ISBN 978 1 84905 952 7
eISBN 978 0 85700 810 7

The Big Book of Dyslexia Activities for Kids and Teens
100+ Creative, Fun, Multi-sensory and
Inclusive Ideas for Successful Learning
Gavin Reid, Nick Guise and Jennie Guise
ISBN 978 1 78592 377 7
eISBN 978 1 78450 725 1

Fun Games and Activities for Children with Dyslexia
How to Learn Smarter with a Dyslexic Brain
Alais Winston
Illustrated by Joe Salerno
ISBN 978 1 78592 292 3
eISBN 978 1 78450 596 7

Dyslexia is My Superpower (Most of the Time)
Margaret Rooke
Forewords by Professor Catherine Drennan and Loyle Carner
ISBN 978 1 78592 299 2
eISBN 978 1 78450 606 3

**The Illustrated Guide to Dyslexia
and Its Amazing People**
Kate Power and Kathy Iwanczak Forsyth
Foreword by Richard Rogers
ISBN 978 1 78592 330 2
eISBN 978 1 78450 647 6

How Can I Remember All That?

Simple Stuff to Improve Your Working Memory

Dr. Tracy Packiam Alloway

Illustrated by David O'Connell

Jessica Kingsley *Publishers*
London and Philadelphia

First published in 2019
by Jessica Kingsley Publishers
73 Collier Street
London N1 9BE, UK
and
400 Market Street, Suite 400
Philadelphia, PA 19106, USA

www.jkp.com

Library of Congress Cataloging in Publication Data
A CIP catalog record for this book is available from the Library of Congress

British Library Cataloguing in Publication Data
A CIP catalogue record for this book is available from the British Library

ISBN 978 1 78592 633 4
eISBN 978 1 78592 634 1

Printed and bound in Great Britain

MIX
Paper from
responsible sources
FSC® C013056

To Marcus—who drew the inspiration for Tommy and is willing to put working memory tips to the test.

Contents

Preface   10

Introduction   13

1. **Why Can't I Remember All That?**   **18**

2. **Things That Can Be Tricky**   **24**

3. **How Can You Improve Your
    Working Memory?**   **33**

4. **More Tips to Improve Memory
    (Short-Term and Long-Term Memory)**   **45**

Notes for Grown-Ups   49

Additional Resources   54

Recommended Reading, Resources,
Websites, and Organizations   58

Preface

My name is Dr. Tracy Alloway. I am a psychologist and have spent over a decade researching working memory, our ability to remember and process information. I have shared my research all over the world from Japan to Germany, to Norway, to the USA. I've worked with children with attention deficit hyperactivity disorder (ADHD), dyslexia, autism, anxiety, and other difficulties that affect their learning, all of whom may struggle with their working memory. Although I and other psychologists talk about what working memory is and how it works to adults, very few people have spent time explaining working memory from the child's perspective.

So when I was approached to write this book, I was so excited because I could share working memory from a child's viewpoint and in a way kids could understand.

My son Marcus drew this picture,

which inspired David the illustrator's drawings of Tommy, the boy in this book who has working memory issues.

How to use this book—for grown-ups

How Can I Remember All That? is for children and grown-ups to read together. I have written it in two "voices": Tommy's and mine.

Tommy is a boy with working memory problems, and he shares what it is like for him in the classroom and on the playground. If a child you care for or work with has similar struggles, you can take frequent pauses as you read this book together, to discuss with them if they've ever felt or experienced similar things.

What is working memory? It's not the same as IQ! IQ tests are a way to measure how smart we are. Both IQ and working memory are important for learning. A child can have working memory issues and a very high IQ. Or the other way round.

I tested a few hundred children in kindergarten and tracked their school work over six years. I found that your working memory is really important from kindergarten onwards—if you have a strong working memory at kindergarten it can help you do well in school, even six years later! Supporting a child who has working memory issues, who may do less well in things like reading, writing, and math, is very important.

And the good news is that there is a lot that we can do—once we know what signs to look for—as you'll find out in this book.

As we began to understand more about how working memory affects learning, we have also discovered ways to support working memory. Brain training is a growing and exciting new area—there is a lot of evidence of the brain's plasticity: that it can actually change depending on what we do.

As you read this book, you will discover that little tweaks and changes to daily life can make a big difference in supporting working memory.

At the end of the book there is a short section for adults. Here you will find out more about signs and behaviors to look out for in a child that reflect that they struggle with working memory.

There is also information about how you can test for working memory issues and further reading.

Introduction

Introducing working memory

You may be wondering what *working memory* is.

Some people call working memory our *active memory*, because we use it to remember new facts, like the name of a new friend, but also to work with things we already know.

Working memory is also the memory that helps us multitask. We use it to do more than one thing at a time—like listen to our parents and do what they tell us.

Working memory—the brain's Post-it Note

Working memory is like a Post-it Note. We use it to store information that we need to remember.

TOMMY

My name is Tommy and I know that my Post-it Note isn't as big as some of my friends', because I don't always remember things. Like yesterday, the teacher told us what chapters to study for the test, but when I got home, I had already forgotten.

Sometimes when I concentrate really hard, it feels like my Post-it Note gets larger and I can remember so many things. I still remember the time my best friend Sam told me the name of his favorite movie. And that was last month!

Working memory versus long-term memory

You may think that working memory is the same thing as long-term memory. But long-term memory is different. It's like a library where we keep all the things that we have learned, such as memories from our childhood. It also refers to the knowledge that we have gathered over the years, like facts about a country (*the Taj Mahal is in India*), mathematical knowledge (*8 + 2 = 10*), and grammar rules.

We can think of working memory like a librarian who pulls out the facts when we need them. For example, if we are planning a trip to a country that we haven't visited before, working memory learns new facts and then draws on long-term memory to make connections between the new country and a familiar place.

Working memory versus short-term memory

Working memory is also different from short-term memory, which is our memory that only lasts for a brief period, usually a few seconds. We use short-term memory to remember someone's name, a phone number, or a title of a book. We usually forget this information if we don't make an effort to store it in our long-term memory.

Imagine that you are walking to a new school. You lose your way and stop to ask for directions. You repeat the information to yourself so you don't forget. You are using your *short-term memory* to remember these directions.

As you recite the directions to yourself, you look around and match them to the road names. Is this where you make that right turn? Where do you make that second left? Now you are using your *working memory* because you are working with information that you were given.

Working memory in my brain

Each part of the brain has a special job. There is a part of our brain that specializes in working memory. It's in the front and it is called the *prefrontal cortex*. If you touch your hand to your forehead it's almost like you are touching your working memory.

Working memory is a team When we use our working memory,

it doesn't work alone—it works works with different parts of the brain.

Imagine working memory in the brain as being more like basketball than tennis. Here is what happens when you are having a conversation with your friend Sam.

Sam is talking. Your prefrontal cortex is activated—it has control of the ball! Then it gets information and passes the ball to the brain area that deals with language, which is called *Broca's area*. This part of the brain then passes the ball back to the prefrontal cortex so you can answer Sam's question.

It's nice knowing that working memory is a team player, because it means that if we forget a word, the language area of our brain can help us find the right word.

CHAPTER 1

Why Can't I Remember All That?

Working memory—what's your Post-It Note size?

How do we know if someone has working memory problems? If we fall and break a leg, we can see a cast on the leg, but working memory problems are often hidden from family, friends, and teachers.

Even classroom teachers find it hard to spot when kids have working memory problems. Instead, your teacher might think that you are lazy or unmotivated.

They may say things like "You are not trying hard enough" or "Stop playing around and just focus."

TOMMY

I've played brain games at school before. The school psychologist came to our classroom to work with some of us. I got to play with blocks and do puzzles, which I loved. I'm very good at puzzles. My dad and I once put together a 1000-piece jigsaw puzzle in one weekend. He framed it for me and it is in my room now. I feel very proud of myself whenever I look at it.

The school psychologist also asked me lots of questions, like how an apple and an orange are alike. I thought this was silly and wished I could go back to class.

When I asked her what this was for, she said it was an IQ test and it told her how clever I was. I don't think I did very well because I forgot some of the things she said, so I kept asking her to repeat the instructions. She didn't seem very happy about that.

I liked the games where I had to remember things. Most kids my age (seven years old) can only say three numbers in backwards order. Adults can usually say five or six numbers in backwards order—unless they are like my grandpa. He's like me. He can only say three numbers in backwards order.

Would you like to find out what your working memory is like? Let's play a game. Here are some numbers. Remember them in backwards order. Ready?

5—4

Now it's your turn. Say the numbers in backwards order.

Time for the next round.

4—9—2

Your turn again.

The final and hardest round. Say the numbers in backwards order.

6—1—8—5

Working memory tests measure how much *space* we have on our Post-it Note. If we can't remember all those numbers in backwards order, it is not because we don't know our numbers or that we don't know how to count. If we can't remember all the numbers, it is because our working memory space isn't big enough.

So the game is actually a really useful way of checking if someone has working memory problems.

Working memory and impulse control

Imagine that I put a soft, fluffy marshmallow on your desk. How long could you wait before you eat it? Scientists asked young children that same question and told them that if they could wait five minutes without eating the marshmallow, they would get two marshmallows to eat.

This game showed us how well we can use our working memory to control our *impulses*. This is a fancy way to say that we have to resist the urge to do something we really want to do. This is an important skill to have.

You can try out this game yourselves. You could play this game with marshmallows or something else you like to eat!

When we learn to control our impulses, we can focus on what we need to do. Scientists found that children who have this skill do better in school.

TOMMY

I don't really like marshmallows, so I didn't like this game. But some of my friends found it hard to resist eating the marshmallows. Susie, who sits next to me, covered her eyes so she wouldn't eat the marshmallow. Brian was in front of me and he started humming really loudly to distract himself.

Sam especially loves marshmallows. He ate

the marshmallow the minute it was on his desk! I told him that he could have my marshmallow too.

I did very well in this game! But I didn't tell my teacher that it was because I don't like marshmallows.

CHAPTER 2

Things That Can Be Tricky

Working memory in my classroom

Why is it hard to follow instructions in the classroom if you have working memory issues? Because you have to keep many different things in your brain at the same time. You have to remember what the teacher told you *and* you have to carry out these tasks. It's like juggling many balls, and sometimes you drop one of those balls and forget what you are supposed to do.

TOMMY

When I was in kindergarten, I loved school! There were so many fun activities and the teacher was always there to help me if I forgot something.

I don't mind school now but I find it a lot harder to concentrate. Sometimes I close my eyes and try to listen really hard to what my teacher, Ms. Higgins, is saying. But other thoughts come in my head, like games I would like to play, what I will talk to my friends about at lunchtime, oh, and my favorite comic books I'm reading.

My teacher says that she always has to repeat things for me because I never listen. She even called me a dreamer. But I'm not trying to be one. I think she called me that because I got out the wrong book during math class, and I couldn't remember what page number to go to.

My desk used to be in the back of the classroom. Now the teacher has moved me to the front. I still find it hard to keep track

of what she writes on the board. I try to follow what she writes down carefully, but when I read what I wrote down, it doesn't make any sense. I feel like all the words are jumbled.

Like the other day, I was copying from the board and I wrote the title twice in my book. Once I even spelled my name wrong, with only one M instead of two. Oops.

Sometimes I get really frustrated because I want to answer a question. But when I raise my hand, I forget what I want to say. Even my friend Sam teases me and calls me a "sieve" because he says that things always fall out of my head.

Even though I try to remember, it is very hard for me. The classroom assistant asked me why I always look out of the window when we have writing assignments. I didn't want to tell her that it was because I had forgotten what I was supposed to write, so I just didn't say anything.

Working memory and reading

There is a part of working memory that specializes in verbal information. It's called *verbal working memory*. We use our verbal working memory to work with things we hear and read.

Why is working memory so important for reading? Because we use our Post-It Note to keep all the important speech sounds in mind (like the sound that -*at* makes), match them up with the letters on the page, and combine them so we read the words (like joining *c with* -*at* to read the word *cat*).

TOMMY

I'm a great storyteller. All my friends tell me that.

I like to imagine different characters and stories about them. I could spend all day creating scenarios for my characters.

My favorite part is telling my friends the stories I make up. Ms. Higgins said that I should write them down so I don't forget them. I tried that once. But I didn't like how it turned out. I felt that I couldn't really get my ideas on paper. And it was hard to remember how to spell the words. In the end, my story was nothing like what I pictured in my head.

My mom thinks it's funny that I'm so good at telling stories but I don't like reading. She's right. Whenever I have to read aloud in class, I feel like the words are muddled in my head.

Ms. Higgins says that if I talk about what I read, I will remember it. Sometimes she will ask the class questions about what we read. I always put my head down so she won't notice me.

She says that comprehension is important because it shows that we are paying attention during class. But even when I do pay attention, it is hard for me to remember everything. I spend all my effort trying to read the words and I don't always understand what they mean.

Even when I was young, I never liked to read. I didn't like nursery rhymes either because the words all sounded the same. It was very confusing.

But I loved looking at the pictures. I could spend hours staring at my picture books. Maybe that is why I'm so good at drawing.

So now I try to draw out my stories like a comic book. That way I don't have to worry about using the right grammar or how to spell the words. I can tell my story the way I like. Maybe one day I will be a famous writer of graphic novels!

Working memory and learning numbers

Mathematics also uses working memory, but a different type of working memory. It is called *visual working memory*, and it is like having a chalkboard in our head. Some children close their eyes and see the numbers in their head when they solve a number problem.

To find out more about what our brain is doing when we solve number problems, scientists put children in a special machine called a functional magnetic resonance imaging (fMRI) machine that would "read" their brain!

The children were using a special part of the brain called the *hippocampus* while they were solving mathematics problems. The hippocampus is the home of long-term memory, where we store facts that we have learned. It is shaped like a seahorse; *hippocampus* is derived from *hippokampus*, the Greek word for "seahorse," after all.

45÷9=?

23+169=?

The scientists found that the children in their study didn't have to count when they were solving number problems. Instead they had saved all the number facts in their brain so they could just use their hippocampus to quickly solve the problems.

Imagine that your teacher has given you timed multiplication drills. If you have already memorized your times tables, then you don't even have to use your working memory—your hippocampus will give you the right answer.

When we solve math word problems, we use working memory together with our hippocampus. Working memory helps us understand the problem and the hippocampus gives us the math facts.

Working memory and self-esteem

Children with working memory difficulties can have low self-esteem, which means that you do not think highly of yourself and do not feel confident.

In my job as a psychologist, I studied over 3000 school children and found that this is true! Kids with working memory issues often do have low self-esteem. But what I found out in this study was that they only had low confidence for what they could accomplish. The interesting thing was the children still had a good sense of overall self-esteem and felt a strong sense of belonging with their friends.

It is easy to feel discouraged if you feel that you can't complete an assignment in class or part of your homework. You may start thinking that maybe you aren't very smart because you are trying really hard but still keep forgetting things.

But the good news is that scientific studies are showing us that there are so many different ways to build and strengthen our working memory.

There are lots of great tips in the next chapter!

CHAPTER 3

How Can You Improve Your Working Memory?

Tip 1. Eat

Cacao is good for working memory because it has *flavonoids*. Flavonoids are like the Superman of foods![1] They give your brain a boost, and they are especially good for working memory. High-quality chocolate, with 70 percent or more of cocoa solids, is a good source of flavonoids.

TOMMY

I love all kinds of chocolate, except white chocolate because that is not real chocolate.

---

1 Flavonoids are phytonutrients (plant chemicals) that act as powerful antioxidants (substances that may prevent or delay some types of cell damage) and they give vegetables and fruits much of their color (like the blue in blueberries). A 2009 review that looked at the results of lots of different studies found that flavonoids can enhance working memory and also protect against memory losses associated with getting older.

I did a science project on cacao beans last year so I know all about how chocolate is made. Chocolate comes from the cacao seed, which is crushed, fermented, and dried. Then the seeds are roasted and cracked open like a nut. These are called cocoa nibs, which sound delicious to me because I imagine them as tiny chocolaty Tic Tacs that I can pop in my mouth!

If a chocolate bar says that it is 70 percent cocoa solids, this means that 70 percent of

the bar is from the cocoa nib paste. The rest is usually sugar. White chocolate doesn't even have any cocoa solids in it! That's why I don't like it.

I want to try dipping kale in chocolate. I think kale tastes stringy and I have to chew so much whenever Mom cooks it. Maybe if it is covered in chocolate I will like it more.

My project on how chocolate is made won third place in our school science fair. So now everyone thinks I am an expert on food. At lunchtime, lots of kids ask me questions about their favorite foods. I try to answer everyone's questions, but sometimes they get mad at me when I tell them that chips aren't really good brain food.

You may be interested to learn that one study found that working memory improved within two hours of eating cacao! People in that study were also very quick when doing tests and didn't make many mistakes. So, you could try eating a little dark chocolate before a test, to boost your own working memory.

Other foods are also high in flavonoids. Blueberries and dark, leafy vegetables like spinach and kale are good too. You can try dipping blueberries in dark chocolate for a snack. It may get a little messy to make, but I think you will like how they taste.

Here are some foods that are rich in flavonoids:

- berries: elderberries, blueberries, blackberries, cranberries, black raspberries
- herbs and spices: dill weed, parsley, sage, thyme
- dark chocolate, minimum of 70 percent cocoa
- vegetables: collard greens, kale, spinach
- black-eyed peas
- green tea, black tea.

Good fats

Some fats are also good for our working memory. The best fats for the brain are the ones called omega-3 fatty acids: they are known as DHA and EPA (or docosahexaenoic acid and eicosapentaenoic acid, if you want to know their long names!). One scientific study found that adults who took omega-3 for six months had better working memory.

Foods containing good fats (DHA or EPA):

- oily fish: mackerel, salmon, sardines, trout, tuna
- venison and lean meats
- DHA-enriched eggs.

Tip 2. Smell

Breathe in rosemary or peppermint oil (ask your parents for help with the use of essential oils!). Scientists have found that just four drops of pure essential oils of rosemary placed in a diffuser improved people's working memory scores, compared with lavender oil, which didn't seem to do anything to help working memory.

The science of this is really interesting.

Our brain sends signals back and forth using chemicals called *neurotransmitters*, to make sure everything is running smoothly.

One particularly important signal or neurotransmitter is called *acetylcholine.*

This messenger chemical plays an important role in keeping us focused and paying attention.

Inhaling rosemary oil may prevent the breakdown (destruction) of acetylcholine by other chemicals in our brains, which allows you to focus your attention for longer. Researchers found that peppermint oil can also improve working memory.

Tip 3. Take off your shoes and go for a run

Our research is the first to show that running barefoot leads to better working memory compared to when we run with shoes, regardless of how fast or hard you run (running speed or heart rate). One of the reasons that barefoot running can improve working memory is because you have to focus your attention to avoid stepping on painful objects! Ouch!

TOMMY

We have a race this Saturday. Our whole school competes and they have food stands and water slides for after the race. Billy says he is going to beat me. He has said that since we were in first grade. But he has never beaten me.

This year he says that he has a secret weapon so he will win. I know what it is. He has new running shoes that light up when he runs. I have a secret weapon too. And that will make me win.

Coach started teaching me how to run barefoot. At first we practiced in the park for five minutes. Then we ran for longer. Soon I was running three miles barefoot in the park. Coach said that new studies from a top university showed how barefoot running could help me run faster. He said when I run barefoot I use less force (because it hurts more without shoes!) and that makes me more efficient when I run.

My dad told me about a news story of how college students were running barefoot because it helped their working memory. I don't really know how running barefoot can be good for working memory, but my dad explained it to me. He said that when you run, oxygen is sent to the brain, especially the prefrontal cortex. When you have more oxygen, it's like extra power so the working memory gets a boost. I don't know how long this boost will last but maybe it can help me remember things when I'm in class too.

When you run barefoot, you also have to pay attention to the ground more so you don't get hurt. My dad says that all this extra attention is like a mini brain workout. So I am training my working memory to focus better. That sounds good, I guess. I just hope this helps me beat Billy at the race on Saturday.

Billy and I race at lunchtime sometimes. My friends think I'm faster than him. Sam always cheers the loudest for me. I've known Sam since kindergarten. He was crying on the first day of school and I gave him my lunch. We have been best friends ever since.

Tip 4. Jump, squat, move!
Some scientists have discovered that we learn information better when we move around compared to when we are sitting down. Maybe your teacher tried this with your class. How did that work out?

Here's what happened to Tommy!

TOMMY

Ms. Higgins is using a new way to teach us math, from Denmark. I had to look up where that is. It's a very small country where Vikings used to live, and Lego was invented there!

So, during math class, we move all the tables and the chairs to the side and sit on the floor. When Ms. Higgins gives us a number problem, we try to make the numbers with our body. Susie thinks she is very good at making numbers, but when she tried to make herself into the number 6, she bumped into Sam and they ended up rolling about on the floor laughing.

I tried to make myself into the number 7 and that was easy, but then I forgot what problem I was supposed to solve. Ms. Higgins thinks that when we move our whole body when we do math, we will learn better. She said we won't even have to use papers and pencils to do math because our brains are working so well. Just like the children in Denmark.

I don't see how we can learn if everyone is bumping into each other and laughing. I was going to tell her this. But I like sitting on the floor instead of my chair so I didn't say anything. And you never know, maybe it will help me remember my numbers a little bit better.

A curious fact about learning sports and working memory

Do we use our working memory to help us learn new movements or skills in sports lessons?

In fact, the opposite is true. When we are learning a new sport, it helps to turn off working memory!

When you are too tired to use your working memory, you can actually learn the sports moves much faster!

This is because we are using our *muscle memory* instead of working memory. When we use working memory to learn sports, it is actually harder. When we use our working memory to remember actions, we can feel overwhelmed because there are so many steps.

But when we are tired, we naturally turn off our working memory. This helps our muscle memory learn the actions so we can remember them better.

So what Tommy's teacher and the Danish teachers were doing—when the kids weren't falling around laughing—was helping children to activate their muscle memories for learning numbers and number sentences. That meant they didn't have to rely on their working memory.

Tip 5. Sleep on it!

Studying for tests or exams makes people with working memory problems especially nervous.

You might worry that you won't be able to remember everything you learned in class. Even when you study really hard, does it all seem to fly out of your head when the test is in front of you?

Here is a clever trick to help you use your working memory better: learn just before bedtime.

Sleep "locks in" what we learn so we won't forget it.

The scientific name for this is the *interference effect*, and what this means is that when we sleep, nothing can interfere with what we have learned so we can remember it for longer.

If you find it hard to remember what you've learned for a test, next time try to study before bedtime. If you get sleepy, draw a chart of what you are reading to help you stay awake.

I hope your dreams aren't filled with charts and schoolwork!

CHAPTER 4

More Tips to Improve Memory

(Short-Term and Long-Term Memory)

Short-term memory

Short-term memory is the space that you have to hold information for a short time. You can think of it as like a holding zone—you won't keep the information in your short-term memory for long, just long enough until you can transfer the information to a piece of paper, your computer, or even your long-term memory.

Quickly look at these letters and try to remember them:

NBCUSAATM

Now try it again:

NBC—USA—ATM

Which time was easier?

> **TIP: Chunk it!**
> Chunking—or breaking up information into smaller sections—is a great way to remember more information.
>
> **ANOTHER TIP: Talk fast.**
> Research has found that when we say things quickly, we can remember more information.

Long-term memory

Long-term memory is when you have to keep information for a long period of time. Some of this information can be kept for years and years, like a memorable birthday, while other memories don't last more than a week. Think of long-term memory as like a library full of books. Some books get read more than others so it is easier to remember which shelf you left them on. With long-term memory, some experiences are better remembered than others because you think about them more. As we get older one of the first things to go is our long-term memory, but we can keep it sharp by keeping information relevant.

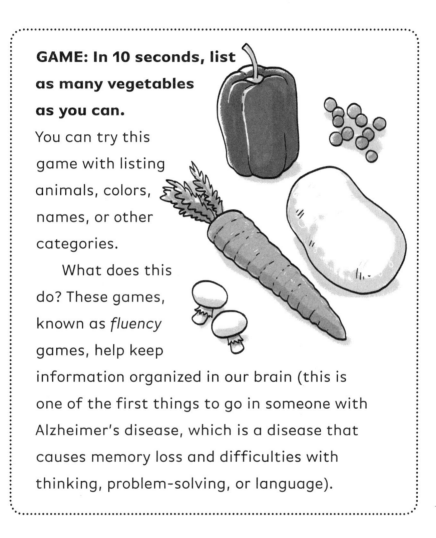

GAME: In 10 seconds, list as many vegetables as you can.

You can try this game with listing animals, colors, names, or other categories.

What does this do? These games, known as *fluency* games, help keep information organized in our brain (this is one of the first things to go in someone with Alzheimer's disease, which is a disease that causes memory loss and difficulties with thinking, problem-solving, or language).

Attention

Sometimes it can be hard to stay alert in the classroom.

ACTIVITY: Doodle! Grab a pencil and tap into your creative side.

Doodling can help you remember things and stay alert. When you doodle while the teacher is talking, it helps things stay in your head.

This "doodling effect" keeps your attention from drifting away—so that you still pay attention instead of daydreaming. Because doodling doesn't require much focus or effort, you can still focus on what you need to do.

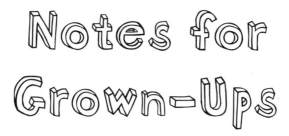

Notes for Grown-Ups

Working memory: quick facts

Here are some key findings from my government-funded projects on the link between working memory and education:

1. Working memory predicts learning success.

Working memory is an accurate predictor of learning from kindergarten to college because it measures *potential to learn*, rather than what has already been learned. In contrast, other measurements like school tests and IQ tests measure knowledge that children have already learned. If students do well on one of these tests, it is because they know the information they are tested on. Likewise, many aspects of IQ tests also measure the knowledge that we have built up.

A commonly used measure of IQ is a vocabulary test. If they know the definition of a word like "bicycle" or "police," then they will likely get a high IQ score. However, if they don't know the definitions of these words or perhaps don't articulate them well, this will be reflected in a low IQ score. In this way, IQ tests are very different from working memory tests because they measure how much students know and how well they can articulate this knowledge.[2]

2. Working memory impacts all areas of learning from kindergarten to college.

Working memory is important for a variety of activities at school, from complex subjects such as reading comprehension, mental arithmetic, and word problems to simple tasks like copying from the board and navigating around school. The importance of working memory in learning is not just limited

---

2 A word of caution about IQ testing. One of my research projects involved two different schools: one was in an urban, developed area, while the other was in an underprivileged neighborhood. As part of the project, students were IQ tested using a vocabulary test. One of the vocabulary words—*police*—drew very different responses. Students from the urban school provided definitions relating to safety or uniforms, which corresponded to the examples in the manual. However, those from the underprivileged neighborhood responded with statements like "I don't like police" or "They are bad because they took my dad away." Although both responses were drawn directly from the children's experiences, only one type of answer matched the IQ manual's definitions. This example illustrates how performance on IQ tests is strongly driven by a child's background and experiences.

to children. A similar pattern can be seen at the university level as well: working memory is a better predictor of grades than college entrance exams like the *Scholastic Achievement Test* (SAT).

3. One in ten students has poor working memory.

In a government-funded study of over 3000 students, I found that ten percent of students had working memory problems that led to learning difficulties in the classroom. That's around three children in a class of thirty. Common working memory problems that children show in the classroom include forgetting instructions, losing their place in an activity, and raising their hand but forgetting what they want to say. You can try the simple test in Chapter 1 in which you remember a three-digit number backwards to see if a child might have working memory issues, then investigate further.

4. A student with poor working memory will not "catch up" with their peers.

Without support, a student with working memory issues will continue to struggle. In a study with high schoolers, I found that teenagers who were diagnosed with working memory problems were still performing very poorly in school compared to peers two years later.

5. Working memory *can* be trained!

Brain training is a growing and exciting new area— there is a lot of evidence of the brain's plasticity: that it can actually change depending on what we do. Clinical trials with Jungle Memory, a working memory training program that I co-developed, demonstrate improvements in working memory, IQ, and learning outcomes. You can find out more about this program here: www.junglememory.com

More strategies to improve working memory at school

Classroom teachers can make small tweaks to the daily routine of the student to support their learning.

1. *Detect working memory failures*. Is the student struggling to keep up with their peers? Are they beginning to disengage from the activity? Are they acting out in frustration? Once you have identified these signs in a student, you can follow the next two recommendations.

2. *Break down information.* If an activity exceeds the working memory capacity of a student, they will be unable to complete the task.

3. *Build long-term knowledge.* This process can foster automaticity of knowledge in the student, which can minimize working memory overload.

4. *Keep it simple.* A new project called "Clever Classrooms" is thought to help students learn better. It includes things like:

    i.   having fewer tables and chairs to give students space to move around
    ii. minimizing information on the walls
    iii. painting one wall a "tranquil" color like light blue
    iv. displaying schoolwork in the hallway to foster a sense of achievement.

Additional Resources

Testing working memory

The Working Memory Rating Scale (WMRS) is a behavioral rating scale developed for educators to help them easily identify students with working memory deficits. It consists of twenty descriptions of behaviors characteristic of children with working memory deficits. Teachers rate how typical each behavior was of a particular child, using a four-point scale ranging from (0) *not typical at all* to (1) *occasionally* to (2) *fairly typical* to (3) *very typical*.

A starting point in developing the items in the WMRS was an observational study of students with poor working memory but typical scores in IQ tests.

Compared with classmates with average working memory, the low memory students frequently forgot instructions, struggled to cope with tasks involving simultaneous processing and storage, and lost track of their place in complex tasks. The most common consequence of these failures was that the students abandoned the activity without completing it.

As the WMRS focuses solely on working memory-related problems in a single scale, it does not require any training in psychometric assessment prior to use.

It is valuable not only as a diagnostic screening tool for identifying children at risk of working memory deficits, but also in illustrating both the classroom situations in which working memory failures frequently arise, and the profile of difficulties typically faced by students with working memory issues.

The scores are normed for each age group, which means that they are representative of typical classroom behavior for each age group.

One item in the WMRS is "needs regular reminders of each step in the written task." The classroom teacher has to rate how typical this behavior is of the student and compare their score to the manual. A five-year-old needs more reminders than a ten-year-old, which is reflected in the scoring of the WMRS. The scoring is color-coded to make it easy to interpret. For example, a score in the green range indicates that it is unlikely that the student has a working memory impairment. If a student's score falls in the yellow range, it is possible that they have a working memory impairment and further assessment is recommended. Scores in the red range indicate the presence of a working memory deficit, and targeted support is recommended.

The WMRS has been validated against other behavior rating scales, such as the Conners' Teacher Rating Scale and the Behavior Rating Inventory of Executive Function (BRIEF) (Alloway, Elliott, and Place, 2010). The WMRS measures behavior that is different from that represented in these other rating scales, and thus reliably identifies students with working memory deficits. The WMRS has also been compared to cognitive tests of working memory, IQ, and academic attainment.

You should also note that the majority of students considered by their teachers to have problematic behaviors (i.e. those typical of students with working memory issues) are more likely to have low working memory scores and achieve low grades (Alloway, Gathercole, and Elliott, 2010).

It is important to know that students who display problematic behavior associated with working memory issues will not necessarily have low IQ scores—many of them can have average IQ scores.

It is working memory overload that leads to all

the behaviors we have discussed, and their loss of focus in the task can make them appear to others to be inattentive and distracted. The WMRS enables teachers to use their knowledge of the student to produce an indicator of how likely it is that the child has a working memory problem. Thus, it provides a valuable first step in detecting possible working memory failures (see www.pearsonclinical.co.uk/Psychology/ChildCognitionNeuropsychologyand Language/ChildMemory/WorkingMemoryRatingScale (WMRS)/WorkingMemoryRatingScale(WMRS).aspx).

Recommended Reading, Resources, Websites, and Organizations

Further reading

Alloway, T.P. (2010a). *Improving WM: Supporting Students' Learning*. London: Sage.

Alloway, T.P. (2010b). *Training Your Brain for Dummies*. Oxford, UK: John Wiley & Sons.

Alloway, T.P. (2014). *Understanding Working Memory*. London: Sage.

Alloway, T.P. (2018). *Working Memory and Clinical Developmental Disorders*. Didcot, UK: Taylor & Francis.

Alloway, T.P. and Alloway, R.G. (2014). *The Working Memory Advantage: Train Your Brain to Function Stronger, Smarter, Faster*. New York: Simon & Schuster.

Alloway, T.P., Elliott, J., and Place, M. (2010). Investigating the relationship between attention and working memory in clinical and community samples. *Child Neuropsychology* 16:242–54.

Alloway, T.P., Gathercole, S.E., and Elliott, J. (2010). Examining the link between working memory behavior and academic attainment in children with ADHD. *Developmental Medicine and Child Neurology* 52:632–6.

Gathercole, S. and Alloway, T.P. (2010). *Working Memory and Learning: A Practical Guide for Teachers*. London: Sage.

Studies mentioned in this book

Cacao study: https://www.frontiersin.org/articles/10.3389/fnut.2017.00019/full

Peppermint study: http://nrl.northumbria.ac.uk/153/1/PeppermintPrePubVersion.pdf

Peppermint: Moss, M., Cook, J., Wesnes, K., and Duckett, P. (2003). Aromas of rosemary and lavender essential oils differentially affect cognition and mood in healthy adults. *International Journal of Neuroscience* 113:15–38.

Numeracy study: https://www.nature.com/articles/nn.3788

Clever Classrooms: https://www.sciencedirect.com/science/article/pii/S0360132315000700

Flavonoids: Macready, A., Kennedy, O., Ellis, J., Williams, C., Spencer, J., and Butler, L. (2009). Flavonoids and cognitive function: A review of human randomized controlled trial studies and recommendations for future studies. *Genes & Nutrition* 4:227–42.

Good fats: Narendran, R., Frankle, W.G., Mason, N.S., Muldoon, M.F., and Moghaddam, B. (2012). Improved working memory but no effect on striatal vesicular monoamine transporter type 2 after omega-3 polyunsaturated fatty acid supplementation. *PLOS ONE* 7:e46832.

Good fats: Tan, Z.S., Harris, W.S., Beiser, A.S., Au, R., Himali, J.J., Debette, S., *et al.* (2012). Red blood cell omega-3 fatty acid levels and markers of accelerated brain aging. *Neurology* 78:658–64.

Rosemary: Moss, M., and Oliver, L. (2012). Plasma 18-cineole correlates with cognitive performance following exposure to rosemary essential oil aroma. *Therapeutic Advances in Psychopharmacology* 2:103–13.

Barefoot running: Alloway, R.G., Alloway, T.P, Magyari, P., and Floyd, S. (2016). Can taking off your shoes be good for your brain? Investigating the effects of barefoot running on working memory. *Perceptual & Motor Skill* 122:432–43.

Move while you learn: http://pediatrics.aappublications. org/content/137/3/e20152743

Doodle: Andrade, J. (2010). What does doodling do? *Applied Cognitive Psychology* 24:100–6.